Why the Moon Only Glows

A Medrash Retold

by Dina Rosenfeld
illustrated by Yehudit Holtzman

Hachai
Publishing

MW01705864

IN HONOR OF OUR BELOVED DAUGHTER

BLIMA AVIVA

FROM YOUR PARENTS
NORMAN AND ELAINE BRODSKY

Copyright © 1992 HACHAI PUBLISHING
ALL RIGHTS RESERVED
This book, or part thereof, may not be reproduced, stored or copied in any form without written permission from the copyright holders, except by a reviewer who wishes to quote brief passages in connection with a review written for inclusion in magazines or newspapers.
THE RIGHTS OF THE COPYHOLDERS
WILL BE STRICTLY ENFORCED.

ISBN 0-922613-00-1 (Hardcover)
ISBN 0-922613-01-X (Softcover)

Printed in Hong Kong

HACHAI PUBLISHING ◆ BROOKLYN, NEW YORK
Tel: 718-633-0100 ◆ Fax: 718-633-0103
www.hachai.com ◆ E-mail: info@hachai.com

Typesetting by
Mendelsohn Press
Brooklyn, N.Y.
(718) 467-1957

A Note to Parents and Teachers

The Biblical description of the creation of the heavenly bodies is a succinct few lines in Genesis:

And G-d made the two great lights
the large light to rule the day
and the small light to rule the night,
and the stars.[1]

The first phrase of this verse implies that G-d created two equally great lights. Why are they referred to in the very next phrase as "large and small"?

Rashi, one of the most fundamental commentaries on the Torah, answers this question with additional details from the Midrash.[2] He writes that the sun and moon were in fact created as identically large and powerful lights. However, the moon objected to being the sun's equal and complained to G-d in the hope that He would diminish the sun's capacity to shine.

For his lack of humility and gratitude, the moon experienced the very thing he had wished upon the sun and was reduced in size and brightness from a blinding light to a soft glow. Therefore, the Torah initially refers to the sun and moon as two great lights, and only after the moon's complaint describes them as "large" and "small."

This Midrash, retold for the very young child, teaches a clear and valuable lesson, namely, that one should be satisfied with whatever he or she has been given, and not begrudge someone else's good fortune. In the end, the moon learns his lesson, and G-d offers the moon some consolation — in the form of stars, to help brighten the night sky.

It is well-known that the Jewish people are compared to the moon.[3] When Moshiach (the Messiah) arrives, both the moon and the Jewish Nation will be restored to their former glory:

"And the light of the moon shall be
as the light of the sun." [4]

May we merit it speedily in our days!

Dina Rosenfeld

[1] Genesis 1:16
[2] Chulin 60, Berashis Rabbah 6:6
[3] Gemorah Sotah 29 Amud 1
[4] Isaiah 30:26

Leah and her brother, Dov, let out a tired sigh
As streaks of orange, red, and pink lit up the evening sky.
Their bikes and balls, their games and dolls,
they'd put back for the day;
They nestled on their pillows to watch daylight fade away.

The room grew dark, but soon the moon, a softly glowing ball,
Cast a beam of hazy light against the bedroom wall.
They said *Shema*, and Leah pulled her blanket to her chin.
“Good night,” said Abba quietly, and gently tucked them in.

"Oh, Abba," whispered Dov, "could you please tell us why it's so
That the sun can shine so brightly, but the moon can only glow?"

"There's a story from the Torah," Abba said, "that tells us why
The sun and not the moon became the brightest in the sky.
I'll tell you how it happened, and then both of you will know
Why the sun can shine so brightly, but the moon can only glow."

◆

When Hashem began to make the world so many years ago,

He first created day and night, then waters high and low.

He made the earth, the dry land, the rivers and the seas,

He then created flowers, and grass and plants and trees.

When the fourth day came, Hashem put up two balls of light so round

A sun and moon, both big and bright, hung high above the ground.

The sun was in its glory, glad to shine up there and share
The job of giving light with moon, and be one of a pair.

But the moon was most unhappy; he was quite dissatisfied.
“Am I the boss, or is the sun? This cannot work!” he cried.
“Two mighty kings are never asked to share a single crown!
One of us should be smaller!” he demanded with a frown.

“Then all will see the bigger one’s the leader in the sky

And know who's best at lighting up the world — the sun or I!"

“A fine idea,” Hashem agreed. “Moon, I think you’re right.
One of you should be small and weak, with soft reflected light.”

Now, who would be the bigger one?
The moon thought that he knew.
“I’m more important than the sun — now I’ll look bigger too!”

Hashem announced , "You did not want to share the sky with sun;
Well, moon, since you complained, you'll have to be the smaller one."

The moon began to shrink and fade; his light grew dim and low.
He cried, “How will I light the night if I can only glow?”

"Please don't feel sad; you've learned your lesson now,"
Hashem replied.
"So I've created tiny stars to twinkle by your side.

They may be little, but they'll join you on the blackest night
And shine away the darkness with their brilliant spots of light."
The moon did not complain or shout, no longer full of pride;
He glowed against the black night sky, small but satisfied.

"And that's the Torah's story," Abba said. "So now you know
Why the sun can shine so brightly, but the moon can only glow."

Abba kissed his boy and girl, then softly closed the door;
The children lay and thought about the moon a little more.
Until their eyes grew heavy and their breathing slow and deep
And with moonlight on their faces,

they drifted off to sleep.

The End

FOR MY MOTHER
WHO ALWAYS SAYS,
"BE SATISFIED."

D.R.

For Mom & Dad
Love,
Judi